just a pause

poetry of mindfulness

by
Joni Staaf Sturgill

ISBN-13: 978-0-692-96256-5

DEDICATION

For my loves, Joey and Mason, and my true love Trevor.
You all mean the world to me and
I'm so thankful for your presence in my life.

Table of Contents

Joni Staaf Sturgill

ACKNOWLEDGMENTS

Thank you to everyone who enjoys and supports my poetry.
Thanks to my editors, my parents, Joe and Joann Jenkins.
I'm grateful for my spiritual home, Kripalu Center for Yoga and Wellness,
where so much of this poetry is written.

Just a Pause

Let's just pause here,
to take it all in.
Look around and feel.
Open your arms and crack open your heart
to the hopeful, bright sky...
Wiggle your feet deep into the earth
in safety.
It's there,
in every moment,
if you pause long enough
to see.
If you can throw fear
to the cautionless wind...
If you dare to let go
of your story...
and risk diving into the honest
bay of your essence...
Safety, faith and love
envelops you,
if you're willing to take
just a pause,
blink open your dark eyes
and accept in the light.

Alive

The forest was alive,
moist breath of earth
rising.
Streams like veins
flowing.
Mane of bright green
swaying.

My breath like the wind,
sighing.
Water from the lake
holding.
Gently rolling clouds,
teasing away patches of blue.

The forest was alive,
from the flirty wink
of the sky
to the whisper, tweet or cry
of the birds...

Rooted tress
calling.
Little critters
scurrying.

I am still.
I am part of it all.
I listen.
I see.
I feel.
I am alive, too.

All of It

Life is love and loss. It's the longing.
It's the chill of uncertainty and the bite of sadness.
It's feeling the feeling without letting it swallow you up.
Positive or not,
The truth is ... it's hard.
We can be grateful.
We can look for the sunshine even
when it hides behind the grey.
We can breathe deeply....
And sometimes it's all still a challenge.
Empty.
Empty.
Or full.
It's both.
Sometimes the gaze is on the empty and sometimes the full.
Your choice
is in how you open your eyes.
Your choice
is in what you want to learn and experience.
Your choice
can be to notice it all,
take it all in,
and to not let it swallow you up.
Life is love and loss. It's the longing.
Just be with it all.
And come home to Love.

The Canyon

It feels like time…
Etched from
passing weather
years gone by.

We hold steady
as the storms
move through us,
Some leaving their mark,
some rinse clean
what's behind.

The depth so still
and the surface...
Change itself.

What do you want
etched on your surface
and what lies at your depth?
The Canyon
doesn't have a choice,
but we do.

In the Simple

Amidst the lyrics to the sad song,
and the story of my chattering mind,
I caught a glimpse of orange butterfly wings
in the bush...
And for a moment, all was quiet.
With such delicate vulnerability,
what else matters?
Nothing...
Just feeling
that gentle presence and
holding space for softness.
It's all around
and within us,
Buried beneath the details
of life's busyness,
to-do lists, chores, memories and worries...
With that flap of orange wings,
it all disappeared...
in the vulnerable, delicate truth
of who we are,
what surrounds us,
what lives deep within us and
what fuels us...
The meaning of life...
Love
...all in the simple flap
of the fragile butterfly wings
I saw that day.

Joni Staaf Sturgill

Life Only Happens Once

I return here for this experience
of forever and never again.
Held in safety by these walls,
protected by this roof
with this view to nourish my soul
and earth's delights to feed my body,
joined in community,
energetically hand in hand
with all those who pass.
Seeking and wandering,
falling and rising,
realigning on the path
forever and never again.

Rhythm

Listen...
Wait to see the waves,
without guessing
where they will land.
There's a rhythm
to our mistakes
and our successes,
a beat, tap, and melody.

I walked the same path
through the same woods
but found it new
each time.
A new song in my heart.
Different words
to describe the same
bright colors,
warm feelings within,
deeper
awareness and awe...

Listen

to feel the rhythm
without resistance.
Go with it...
Beauty in sound and sight
again and again.
Learn the patterns
and open to the changes.
Be here for it all,
and revel in

the experience of utter truth, your truth,
the rhythm of you.

Morning

Sunshine on my face
I smiled at the warmth.
The light shined from outside,
though I felt it emerge from within.
Sunshine on my face
and in my heart.
Warmth inside my soul
expanding into my body.
This life.
This moment.
This breath.
This ray of light...
is me.

The Inside Story

I longed for some deep,
Safe haven,
a place where
I could shelter
from life's noise and storms and heartaches.

Seeking something physical,
The cover of a shade tree,
trust,
A warm blanket to wrap into,
belief,
the arms of another
Who could block out the world,
if only for moments of now.
Love.

That safe haven
Eluded me,
I heard the story that maybe I wasn't worthy.

I wondered, as I gazed into the deep woods,
what lurked in the shadows.

As I grew closer to the darkness,
I found only myself,
my fear,
my past dragging behind.

Hidden under the brush
Amongst the twigs and behind the tallest trees,
I found remnants, pieces
of who I am, who I long to be and
the Fear of getting exactly what I want.

Just a Pause

Deeper still,
I found something more
beautiful than I ever imagined.

The path to the safe haven
is never clear.
It's riddled with stones and ditches and muddy spots.
It curves and it bends and
sometimes I lost my way.
Sometimes, I learned, I must take a chance on faith.

Faith - not something external, not something mystical,
Faith is in me, is in you,
Deep in the woods is a
Safe haven of faith.
of a love that runs fluid and free,
of a love that roots into the earth and reaches for the sky.
Love.

It's the inside story,
hidden by the wet, muddy earth,
the fallen branches,
the sweet scent of pines,
the critters scurrying about and the birds calling overhead.

In our blind spot,
filled by the mind with more noise,
there actually lives a stillness,
a safe haven of trust,
a deep, ever-present love,
and a knowing that everything will be okay.

I awoke to it all,
opened my once clouded eyes
and hooked into this

Inside story.
Love.

Forest Moss

The soft emerald moss
beckoned to my fingers
asking them to feel
what nature offered
in the forest that day.

A marriage of opposites,
she lay her pillow of green
on the cool gray rock,
Wrapping him in warm
Protection.

She breathed with the breeze
and grew thick and deep.
With feathery fronds
and reaching webs,
She rooted on the
grounding rock
and snuggled in.

There in her dim
resting place,
she smiled and received the
forest's blessing.

In the Flow

The little creek
spilled and splashed
down the hill
over the jagged rocks,
to settle
into stillness and reflection...
if only for a pause,
a moment,
a breath...
before flowing on,
trickling further
with the way,
not fighting,
not fearing,
not struggling to climb
back up the mountain,
or resist gravity.
She just flowed,
and held herself steady,
flowed and held steady,
again and again.
Where will the little creek land?
No matter...
she breathed into the journey.

The Life

The life all around me
in the woods
calling out.
Crickets chirping.
Squirrels and chipmunks scurrying.
Birds singing.
The symphony overwhelmed me
to tears
as I paused
my movement,
my thoughts,
my wondering.
I marveled at the life
all around me
in the woods
calling out.
It's here
It's now,
With me or without me,
and so
I joined in their song,
I joined in
the life
in the woods,
We were one.

The Little Ant

The little ant crawled
over rocks that
must have been boulders.
under twigs,
as the biggest fallen trees.
On he went,
Exploring.
Turning and crawling.
Stillness and movement,
along the root
of a majesty.
Up a blade of drying grass,
and down again.
No rhyme,
Just wandering.
Moving through, over and around
Whatever lies ahead,
He marches on.

Creek on the Mahkeenac

The dry creek bed,
exhausted from the constant flow
had no more tears to cry.
No more to carry away,
And so she stopped.

She knew it was time
for a change,
So she let the earth
be quenched.
She gave every last drop.

When the final trickle
dried on her tear-stained body,
a creek she was no longer.
She was birthed into
a beautiful etching
on the earth's skin.

Something new
for now…
with a future unknown.
She sighed
and stretched out,
accepting, opening, smiling
into rock and dirt.
Her path, like ours…
limited, uncertain and
a blessing to be shared.

It's to do with Fear

Don't fear the fear, he said.
Keep going.
Even when the ground beneath you shakes.
Even when no answers, and the right questions elude you.
Don't fear the fear.
Feel it and keep going.
Life leads you to your growth,
Life leads you to your love,
Life leads you to walk through
the fire of your fear and truly live.
Keep going.
Feel the fear
and step into being here anyway.
Don't fear the fear, he said.

The Space

What is this space inside?
This hole in my heart?
why does it ache and squeeze
so much
sometimes that
tears burst from my eyes,
uncontrolled?

Connection.
What we all desire.
when they're not here they're still with me,
My teachers' voices ring in my head,
Separateness is an illusion.
Those who are part of us,
are part of us.
Always present.
We are all, in fact, connected.

Then why do I feel this sadness
this loneliness...
When my loves
leave,
be it for a short time
or forever?

Why does it ring
So hard and so loud?
Why does the squeeze feel so tight
and the liquid fear drip from my eyes?

Is this part of the ride?
Am I to figure this out?
And how will I feel tomorrow?

One step at a time, I'll move
through this hole in my heart,
perhaps simply exploring it,
looking at the edges,
the color, the shape...
Maybe it's not about filling it up,
but accepting its presence.
Accepting that the hole will always be there in one form or another.

I know this to be true,
And I exhale a sigh,
As the hole squeezes me
and saltwater streams from my eyes
once again.

Onward

The wind at my back
Urging me forward on the path
I knew was mine
The path I was meant to walk
Stuck in the mud of inaction
I was no longer.
Forward with the waves as they
Crash to shore
Forward as the sun stretches across the sky
One step at a time...
Holding fear by the hand gently
Saying it's ok,
Let's go anyway.

Empathy

Can you hear babies cry?
They cry
when there's something wrong.

Do you hear me?
Can I stop my chatter
to truly listen to you?
Can we
feel each other's tears?

So wrapped up in our own thoughts,
we can't stop our spiral…
We can't
open our hearts and try to understand
what the cry is about.
Maybe we can help
and maybe we can't.
But we can
Listen.
to each other and those
we do not understand.

For it is the only way to learn.
To consider another's perspective,
To truly
Listen.

What is hidden deep within, that we don't even see?
What do we avoid turning our eyes to?
And why?
Look at it all,
it's you.
Look,

it's me.
And it's ok.
Life is falling and rising.
Learning and losing
Pain is part of it.

Feel and empathize.

Here

We sheltered under the trees,
close to the lake's edge,
While the sky's light
Shined
new awareness,
connection,
safety...
The shower
cleansed us
of our old patterns
and opened us up
to possibly.
It washed away
fears
and the chatter of the mind
in those moments.
So we walked
and we talked.
We soul gazed into ourselves,
and held human hands.
The time came to say
goodbye
and we stopped
to breathe.
We parted,
not knowing
what's to come,
but
we smiled anyway.

Strong Enough

I said I was strong
like the rooted maples and oaks
in the forest.
So I was...
even when the tears flowed like a spring,
even when I fell to the earth in defeat.

The forest floor held me so gently,
cradling my fallen hopes,
and drawing out my sorrow.

Underneath it all,
I said I was strong.

I'd been here before,
Weeping and Sleeping
blindly beneath the shade trees,
sinking into the mud.
Heavy with thought and carrying a needless load.
One drop at a time I released it to the earth.
And the forest consumed it...
like it methodically ingested
autumn's crispy leaves
from now budding branches.

The internal wave came.
Grey clouds showered me
with awareness
and I woke, gasping for air
With the cry of a baby's first breath.
I could begin again.
And I knew I was strong enough
to do just that.

The Oak Trees

With a touch to the
rooted giant,
I let go
of anything that held me back.
I felt it rise
up and out of me.
The footed beast
could hold it and send it down
to the earth's fire
and free me.
So I sat,
grounding myself.
Becoming part of the forest,
if only for moments.
Leaves floated down
brushing by,
paying me no mind.
The oak and her friends
Swayed
with the cool breath
of the day
and whispered a song
of strength and resilience.
It'll all be okay.
It'll all be okay.
It'll all be okay.
So says the oak trees.

My Fire

The fire rose up in me
to breathe joy,
to breathe life,
to dance my heart,
to shine my soul…
And I was seen,
and I was known
in this heated way…
I didn't want to douse
the blaze, but fan the flames
and be warmed and enraptured by them.

Mindful On The Bench

Wood beneath my fingers.
Earth beneath my feet.
Voices and bird calls echoed around
and I breathed.
I sat on this bench
and let it all pass by.
The wind through my hair,
The sun on my face,
The plop in the water…

Wood beneath my fingers.
Earth beneath my feet.
The simple present
I breathed,
and let it all pass.
Quiver and rustle of the leaves,
Call of the geese,
Humming in the distance,
Oars rowing on the water.

Wood beneath my fingers.
Earth beneath my feet.
I am still on this bench,
living right now
and I feel peace.

Love

Thank you universe
for blessing me with so much love,
love in the form
of the warm sun on my face
love in the crisp wind,
awakening me to this moment,
Deep green love of the grass and
blooming ferns in the Spring woods.
Love in my body
Love in my heart
Love with the souls
who touch my life with
friendship and connection.
Grateful for love,
Lit up by love,
overflowing with love,
feeling love here and now,
and waiting for love.

True beauty

Beauty in the sun.
Beauty in the rain.
In the clear blue and the cloudy.
In the light and dark.
Even in the anxious faces
of those who don't see.
We are the authors
of our story,
though we forget.
We can see
the beauty all around or
the misery.
What we wish it to be...
or reality.
All the times I cried here,
I shed my skin.
All the grief over
a life I didn't plan,
I didn't see.
What if I just lived
what I have?
Finally I see
and all is bursting
around me...
With life as it is,

I finally see
True Beauty.

My Favorite Thing

"What's your favorite thing about life?" he asked.

My favorite thing about life...is this moment.

It's seeing the flow of moments tied together with hope and expectation, only to unravel and turn a drastically different way.

It's being here and in the next moment with curiosity and wonderment, sampling spoons of honey from each circumstance, and sometimes wailing with sorrow and being present for that pain...Savoring the juxtaposition between the two. It's being in nature and understanding the connection from which we all come...feeling the warm sun on your skin or the rain move your body from dry to dripping wet... it's seeing the seasons change, the leaves bud with new growth, then fill with green, then dry and fall.

Savoring each bite, each morsel of experience.

What's my favorite thing about life?

My favorite thing is when questions like these connect mind to heart, and as the heart opens, you get to know your soul, and as your soul shines forth from your body, you feel lit up from the inside out...You feel Love from the tips of your toes to the turned up corners of your mouth and your eyes...You feel fearless...or you feel fear and want to stretch your arms wide and open anyway.

Ashes

In the dance,
I lit my fire,
my flow,
my spirit, and
I wondered how my demons
could be set free.
With the sudden step of my feet,
the swivel of my hips,
the spin of my being,
I was quenched.
I let go.
To ashes, it all dropped,
In the dance.

Spring Smile

Wet green grass at my feet,
so bright.
I stood,
hugged by a silvery fog.
It enveloped my moment and
freed my mind to be here now.

I breathed in the
Fragrant birth of morning.

I closed my eyes and listened to
the rain dance joyfully
atop my red umbrella…
a celebration of release,
a rejoice in tears,
Certainty at the pattern,
The flow
The journey.

The corners of my mouth turned up
breathing in the
sweet growth of Spring.

Squirrel Play

Following the squirrel
playful on his path,
with the same delight...
Curious
without sound,
Dancing
Collecting
nuggets of nourishment...
Feeling the earth beneath,
and the crisp air all around.
The squirrel knows.
It's Fall.

With Each Footfall

Step by step.
That's all we can do.
Can't jump from here to there,
but only
one foot in front of the other.
Sometimes...
that's all there is.
This step and the next.
Breathe into it,
Laugh,
Be curious,
And drop
whatever is behind you.
Look only a few
paces forward and now.
Lighten with each footfall,
and you'll be free.

Motherhood

I process my experiences
through metaphor and poetry,
I understand life more deeply
if I can paint a picture with words.
But I've never written
about motherhood before.
I write about all of my human emotions…
ones that touch me deeply,
ones that create profound joy and sorrow.
But never have I written
about the experience of being a mother.
Yet this is such a huge part of my life,
of my existence,
of my purpose on this earth...
to be the mother of my two boys
whom I love more
than I can express with words.
That's it,
I've never written about motherhood
because I simply cannot express
the magnitude
of emotion and
feeling and
embodiment of experience
around this gift,
this blessing,
this interwoven part of my existence.
There aren't enough words to explain
the depth and the soul
and the worry and the love
and the connection
I've experienced being a mother.
It is the thing I am most grateful
for in life...this experience

of giving birth to and
journeying with life itself.
Blessing beyond blessing
connection beyond connection
I'll take this with me forever.
I love you, Joey and Mason
more than I will ever be able
to express in words.
I love you from the tips of my being
to the depth and center,
I am grateful in an expensive way
that explodes from my overflowing heart
to the tears in my eyes,
at the journey of
Motherhood.

Giggled with Delight

Blooming buds
on the apple tree
burst with hope
and danced
on Spring's breath.
Not knowing
Not caring
if they will bear fruit.
Instead,
they giggled with
delight
in the moment.
I danced to do the same.

Beginner's Mind

I opened my eyes and
saw beauty
in the simple.
Faces, eyes and insecurities
that weave a human fabric
of growth edges and
blocks.
One little wiggle
and the next.
Touch the earth
through the floor.
Feel ribs expand with a little
Breath
then more, and more.
I opened my eyes
and felt truth
Inside and out.
Could look it in the eye
and give it a warm embrace,
Learning something
each moment I can see...
With beginner's mind

On the Lake

Early morning sun
Sparkled on the lake
and I felt it in my heart.
Glittering with joy
as the water shifted and carried
The light
this way and that way,
without hesitation
or plan...
It twinkled
and I smiled because
I knew it was inside me, too.
This calm flow
This light
This dancing joy.
I am the depth of the lake
and the reflecting light.
I am the breath and the sunlight.
I am the joy
in that moment,
on the lake.

Delight

The sound of my boots on
the wet sandy path...

Soaked leaves

The tapping of raindrops
on my umbrella...

Honking of geese
Squeak of the chipmunks
Tweet of the finch

Such delight!

Who are we to choose
and want to control?

Why not allow
and sparkle with delight?

Intimacy

It's not a physical act,
it's not done with just the body,
It is knowing
something special,
sharing mind, soul, emotion, and body...
it's truly looking,
seeing and being seen,
knowing and being known,
without judgment,
but with tender hands and heart...
it's holding gently,
it's squeezing tightly,
gazing deeply,
feeling like you know
every curve,
every bump,
every soft spot,
every scar
in someone's heart,
someone's soul,
in a special way...
with a special language that only the two of you speak.

Modern Dating

Wearing suits of expectation,
they smiled and tried to connect.

Thick layers tried to touch
each other
and they wondered why they couldn't feel.

Without a thought or a breath
they turned their backs

to greet another,
layered with yet more armor.

They continued
to superficially glance,
Then turn away.

Look, then leave...
and their layers
of fear and resistance to change
grew thicker

Their hearts lonelier.

Always searching,
but never opening eyes
Fully enough to truly see.
Never opening hearts
to fully feel,

"It's too vulnerable,
I'll get hurt!"
And so the wall

grows thicker and
connection grows weaker.
Soon,
even the idea,
the spark,
the notion
of deep, connected,
old-fashioned, romantic
Love
dies.

And here I sit,
with a big dumb open heart
hopeful.

in a sea with walls
and armor, I wait

for the warrior without
his costume of false protection.
I wait for his truth
and I wait for love.

Grounded & Free

I was grounded,
Rooted maybe for the first time.
The willow trees
wept with me no longer,
instead we danced in the cool wind…
We danced in the rain…
We danced in the warm sun…
And I felt free.
Free enough to fly with the birds,
yet rooted like the oldest trees
in the deep woods.
I flowed with the stream.
I balanced like the rock cairn.
I could still cry with the rain
but I felt peace.
Peace with my tears,
with my frustration,
with my laughter,
with my wisdom and my joy.
It's all here…
It's all on the journey
and it's all okay.
It's food for the soul.
Puzzles for the mind.
Feelings for the heart.
Movement and stillness for the body.
And I love every moment.
Grounded and free.

The Moment

The light in your eyes
made me see…
You and who you are.
As if I'd known you forever.

The fire in our lips
when they came together...
We lit up the darkened sky
that night.

When you wrapped me
in your arms

After we laughed
and we talked about everything.
I heard you…
I saw you.
And we lit up the darkened sky.

I breathed in
the feeling that I'd wondered
if my heart could feel.

Like a warm rain washing
away my sad story

I became present to potential again.
I breathed in

the light we shared
when I saw you
when I knew you.
When we lit up the darkened sky
that night.

We Soared

Riding the wind
we soared
through the blue...

Opening hearts and hands
to hold the space
between...

Until our lips meet again
and hearts can wrap
in warm embrace...

The whisper of the wind
called us together,
It sang a sweet tune...

and we danced...
our gaze,
our bodies,
our connection...

Soaring through the blue
hands held on hearts
holding space

breathing this beautiful moment
and more,
riding the sky...
and the wind as it blows.

Hands Held on Hearts

He placed his hand
on my heart.
I love you.
I felt it
long before
the words were spoken.
I knew.
from the connection I felt
instantly in his arms,
to our deep gaze,
through the journey
of learning...
how deeply we felt,
and how much we shared.

A "never-before" experience,
a magnetic pull
we return to again and again,
hands on hearts,
through highs and lows.
a sigh of breath
into passion and comfort,
into friendship and love.
as if there were no beginning and no end.
Our journey,
dancing
with laughter and ease,
hands held on hearts.

Swayed

I offered an open hand to the sky…
And the wind carried me
through
whispering mornings
and wailing gusts.
I let it carry me through a storm…
And it dropped me
into stillness.
I realized it was
just a change of direction,
a shift in my course
that led me by surprise,
to just where I needed to be...
I found myself in the arms
of true love.
Together, we swayed
with the wind's breath
and danced.

Every Pore

I breathed it into
every pore,
every cell,
every electromagnetic spark
of who I am.

The crystal clear
feeling of
Light,
Love, and
Contentment.

The moment wasn't perfect.
It wasn't,
by some's standards,
even anything
interesting..

But in a flash
I felt the
Light
Flow into
every pore
every cell,
every electromagnetic spark.

It filled me to the top...
Until I had no choice
but to smile,
to laugh,
and invite it to sink
Deeper...

Into Love

that radiated
from my bones to
the softest touch
of skin.

Love that
I felt
In every pore
every cell
every electromagnetic spark
Of my whole being.

And finally...
I felt I could rest
in contentment.
It rooted and entangled softly
in my nervous system,
in my head and my heart.
Finally...
I was at ease in my soul.

The Jet Stream

Is that the sound
of you
coming home to me?
The fading roar overhead
and
the trail in the sky.

Our hearts coming home...
through the jet stream.

Even when you're far,
I feel you…
I know you…
We are forever connected
Like the wind and the sky,
Like the rain and the sun,
the night and the day...

So close and so far.
Entangled, my love.

Our hearts coming home
through the jet stream.

Separate but One

He is in my heart
always
with me.
We held hands and walked,
though he was miles away.
Felt his hand on my heart
and the depth of warmth
and love
it offered.
And I know he felt me.
We lived and breathed
connected
by some indescribable force,
a spiritual hand,
a whispered entanglement,
where we are separate
but one.
"I love you," I spoke to the wind.
"And I love you," my heart answered
in his voice.
He is in my heart,
always with me.
My love.

Pine Needle Rain

Evergreen scent
filled us to the top
and we smiled
into the forest
and each other's eyes.

Earth and sky
kissed so intimately
that day,
when the pine needles
rained down.

Sunlight glittered
on leafy tree tops
and the breeze
scattered light.

All was quiet
when we gazed up
at our green canopy,
except for the sound
of the pine needles
raining down.

Mossy, fallen trees
graciously aged
and melted into
their return to the soil.

We breathed in
the light and the peace
holding hands,
wrapped in love...
Our lips pressed together

Just a Pause

as the pine needles
rained down.

My Damaged Heart

In the cold, clean room,
when my blood came back,
the man in grey sat down.

He said my heart,
my heart had been damaged.

Inside I thought
of all the times
I'd been hurt so deeply,
of all the times
I gave everything but something
didn't work,
of all the times
I told myself I wasn't good enough,
of all the lessons I'd learned
and tears I'd cried.

Yes, of course my heart,
My heart
has been damaged.

I turned and I looked into
the eyes of my love,
who I feel so deeply,
who snuggled in by my side
and held my hand so tight...

"I don't want to be alone,"
the words just slipped
from my mouth,
as fear trickled
from my eyes.

He squeezed more,
"You are not alone.
You will never be alone."

There he is,
the love of my life,
out here...
but he is also inside me,
Repairing my heart,
as we speak...
as he had been,
since the moment we met.

He has shown me love
in the purest sense:
seeing me deeply...
more than my body,
understanding me...
knowing my inner voice,
feeling me...
my heart, my fear, and my love,

He is present,
even when he's away.

Divine love
in human form,
connection
ever-present,
entangled,
illuminated.

Sent to show me,
to show us both
Truth and Love.

To show us,
that no matter what,
we are under
an umbrella of protection,
and everything's going to be okay.

My heart has been damaged?
Yes, it has.
Life does that to us.

But I trust in
the strength of my heart,
and I trust in
Love.

Love in the garden
of my body and mind
that I'm tending.

Love from the universe
that swims deep in us all.

And Love from
this human being
who is here to help
Open my eyes,
so together we can
stitch and repair
the damaged spaces
in my heart and in his...

So they can beat more fully
to the rhythm and the songs
we create in this life,
so we can dance as
we are meant to dance,

healing our hearts.

All this,
I received
in the unexpected blessing...
sitting in the cold, clean room,
when my blood came back,
and the man in grey sat down
to tell me about my damaged heart.

When Words Aren't Enough

There aren't enough words,
he said,
to describe what my heart
is bursting to say.
I agreed.

Still we tried.
Colors seem brighter,
the sky is bigger,
my heart is more full
than I ever thought possible.
He smiled into my eyes.

Entangled and free,
within the roots and wings
of connection,
we created something more
than the complete beings we were
on our own.

Something so soulful,
so deep and round and
full and woven,
that sometimes I wonder
how there was a time
when we weren't together.

There aren't enough words,
I said.
So we gaze into each other's eyes.
We hold hands and touch,
our lips in magnetic captivation.

We love,

Love as a verb
and not just some fleeting feeling of the heart.
We love,
as though we are plugged into each other
and what surrounds us.
We love
by coming home to each other's
bodies, hearts, minds and souls
and taking refuge from the world
in that tenderness.

There aren't enough words,
we said.

And we sought the description
in every experience:
a trip to the store,
a hike in the deep woods,
sharing a delicious meal,
in a moment surrounded by others,
in the soft and rough edges of earth and sky,
of talk and touch,
of silence and perception,
of love and love and love.

And so we ride the waves of
wonder and curiosity,
allowing love to enfold us
again and again.

No need to wish for
another sunset when we are living
in the awe and beauty and breath
of such clarity.

Joni Staaf Sturgill

There aren't enough words,
and so we laughed.
We kissed.
We danced.

About The Author

Joni Staaf Sturgill has been studying mindfulness techniques for nearly 20 years, and teaching in the Pittsburgh area for 14 years. She holds an MS in Counseling Psychology, BA in Communication, and has advanced training in mindfulness and yoga (ERYT-500). She studied at the Institute for Integrative Nutrition and the Kripalu School of Yoga. Through her business, *Healthy Body Peaceful Soul*, she shares insights on mental, emotional and physical wellness to corporate populations, educational institutions, cancer patients, students of her training programs, and other various groups and individuals. Joni can be reached via her website, www.healthybodypeacefulsoul.com. Just a Pause is Joni's second poetry book. Her first, Heart of All Life, reached #2 on Amazon's hot new releases in poetry by women.

www.ingramcontent.com/pod-product-compliance
Lightning Source LLC
Chambersburg PA
CBHW071424040426
42445CB00012BA/1285